STORMS
TORNADOES

by Jim Mezzanotte

Reading consultant: Susan Nations, M.Ed.,
author/literacy coach/consultant in literacy development

Science and curriculum consultant: Debra Voege, M.A.,
science and math curriculum resource teacher

Please visit our web site at: garethstevens.com
For a free color catalog describing Weekly Reader® Early Learning Library's list
of high-quality books, call 1-877-445-5824 (USA) or 1-800-387-3178 (Canada).
Weekly Reader® Early Learning Library's fax: (414) 336-0164.

Library of Congress Cataloging-in-Publication Data

Mezzanotte, Jim.
  Tornadoes / by Jim Mezzanotte.
    p. cm. — (Storms)
  Includes bibliographical references and index.
  ISBN-13: 978-0-8368-7916-2 (lib. bdg.)
  ISBN-13: 978-0-8368-7923-0 (softcover)
  1. Tornadoes—Juvenile literature. I. Title.
  QC955.2.M49   2007
  551.55'3—dc22   2006033924

This edition first published in 2007 by
Weekly Reader® Early Learning Library
A Member of the WRC Media Family of Companies
330 West Olive Street, Suite 100
Milwaukee, WI 53212 USA

Editorial direction: Mark Sachner
Editor: Barbara Kiely Miller
Art direction, cover and layout design: Tammy West
Photo research: Diane Laska-Swanke

Photo credits: Cover, title, © Tim Samaras/Weatherpix Stock Images; pp. 5, 6, 9, 12 © Weatherpix Stock Images; pp. 7, 10 Scott M. Krall/© Weekly Reader Early Learning Library; p. 11 © Eric Nguyen/Jim Reed Photography/Photo Researchers, Inc.; p. 13 © Joseph Golden/Photo Researchers, Inc.; p. 15 NOAA; p. 16 © Jim Reed/Photo Researchers, Inc.; p. 17 © AP Images; p. 19 © Howard Bluestein/Photo Researchers, Inc.; p. 20 © Eric Nguyen/Jim Reed Photography/CORBIS; p. 21 © Tom Bean/CORBIS

Printed in the United States of America

1 2 3 4 5 6 7 8 9 10 10 09 08 07 06

Table of Contents

Cover and title page: A tornado blows stacks of hay into the air above this Kansas farm field. Kansas sometimes gets more than one hundred tornadoes a year.

CHAPTER 1

Get Ready for a Twister!

The sky is dark with storm clouds. Suddenly, you hear a roaring sound. A tube-shaped cloud stretches to the ground. Watch out! It is a tornado!

A tornado is a strong wind that spins in a circle. It is also called a twister. It can flatten houses and send cars flying. When a tornado hits, people may get hurt or killed.

Tornadoes move in a zigzag path. We cannot guess where they will go! They can travel across the ground as fast as a car. Their twisting winds can spin up to 300 miles (480 kilometers) an hour.

Some tornadoes last a few minutes. Others last more than an hour. They mostly hit during **thunderstorms**. Rain or **hail** may fall, too.

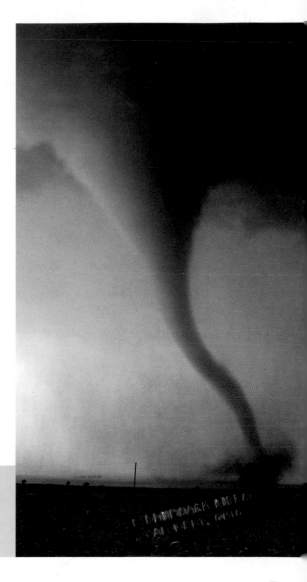

The sky grows darker as a tall twister cuts a path across Kansas.

Most tornados are shaped like a **funnel**. The bottom can be about 500 feet (150 meters) wide. Sometimes, it is much wider.

Tornadoes can be loud. The rushing winds make a roaring sound. A tornado can sound like a jet plane, a rocket, or a train.

The funnel of a tornado spins toward a South Dakota farm.

6

Many places get tornadoes, but the United States gets the most. It gets about one thousand each year! Tornadoes often hit states in the center of the country. This area is called Tornado Alley.

Tornadoes mostly hit southern states in the spring. They mostly hit northern states in the summer. But tornadoes can happen any time of year.

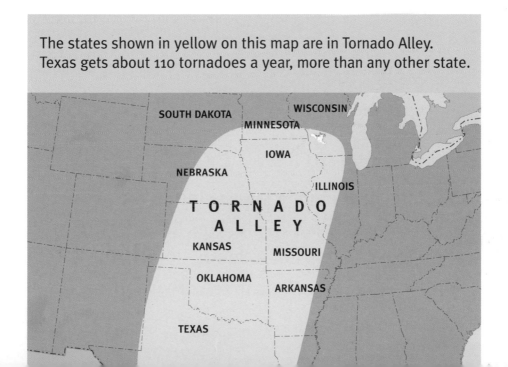

The states shown in yellow on this map are in Tornado Alley. Texas gets about 110 tornadoes a year, more than any other state.

SOUTH DAKOTA
WISCONSIN
MINNESOTA
IOWA
NEBRASKA
ILLINOIS
T O R N A D O
A L L E Y
KANSAS
MISSOURI
OKLAHOMA
ARKANSAS
TEXAS

CHAPTER 2

How Tornadoes Form

Tornadoes begin in big storm clouds. The clouds start to form with warm air. This air is full of water. The water is not a liquid. It is a **gas** called water **vapor**. We cannot see water vapor.

Warm air always rises. Higher in the sky, the air and vapor cool. The vapor turns into drops of water. These drops join together and form clouds.

More air rises and cools. The clouds get larger and darker. They are full of water drops. The drops get heavier. They begin to fall as rain.

Most storm clouds are wider at the top than at the bottom. This storm produced a tornado one hour after this photo was taken.

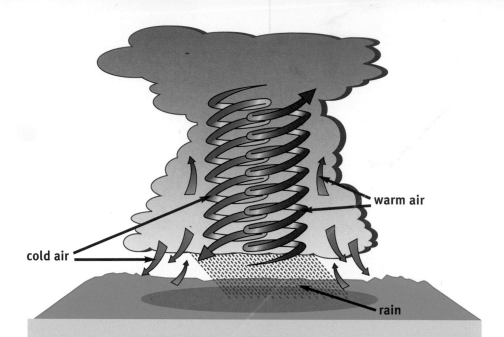

warm air

cold air

rain

Inside a storm cloud, the rising warm air (*red arrows*) and falling cold air (*blue arrows*) start spinning together.

The rain pulls down cold air. The cold air meets the rising warm air. The warm air and cold air twist around. The clouds begin turning.

Part of a cloud grows downward. A tube of spinning air reaches down even farther. It already has a tornado's funnel shape.

The funnel is like a big **vacuum cleaner**. It keeps sucking in warm air. The funnel gets longer. It gets closer to the ground.

A funnel cloud starts to form during this storm in Kansas. The storm also produced hailstones the size of softballs.

A tornado destroys the small town of Manchester, South Dakota. A half-mile wide, the tornado sucked up houses, trees, and dirt.

When the funnel touches the ground, a tornado is born! It is dark from the dirt and other things it sucks up from the ground.

Strong winds rush toward its center. Things that get sucked into it get thrown back out. They fly away from the tornado at high speeds. A tornado ends when it lifts from the ground.

Sometimes, a funnel moves across a lake or sea. Then, it becomes a **waterspout**. Water gets sucked into the funnel.

Most waterspouts are smaller and weaker than tornadoes. But they can damage boats.

Waterspouts are not as wide as tornadoes on land.

CHAPTER 3

Deadly Tornadoes

Tornadoes cause disasters in some places.
Big tornadoes often hit Bangladesh, a country
in Asia. Tornadoes have destroyed many
homes there.

In the United States, the worst tornado hit in 1925. It was named the Tri-State Tornado. It lasted more than three hours. It traveled more than 200 miles (320 km).

First, the tornado hit Missouri. Then, it sped through Illinois and Indiana. It wiped out whole towns. It killed almost seven hundred people.

The Tri-State Tornado hit this building in Illinois.

Tornadoes pick up and throw things with great force. This water cooler was pushed through a wooden door by a tornado in Texas.

During a tornado, strange things happen. A house gets moved down the street. People and animals are thrown in the air. They land far away. Sometimes, they are not even hurt!

A waterspout can suck fish from water and drop them on land. People think it is raining fish!

After a tornado hits, the cleanup begins. People rebuild their homes. A tornado may cut a narrow, zigzag path. One house may be flattened, but the house next door may be fine.

Tornado wind speeds are hard to measure because the powerful winds break the measuring tools. Scientists look at the amount of damage a tornado did to know how fast its winds were.

Broken roofs and walls are all that remain of homes torn apart by a tornado. Other houses on the street are not damaged at all!

CHAPTER 4

Tornado Safety

Scientists try to decide if a twister is coming. They watch for new thunderstorms. They use **radar** to study the storms. They use pictures taken from space, too.

The scientists may decide a tornado could hit. They may learn that a tornado has been spotted. Then, they warn people.

Television and radio stations give the warnings. In some places, sirens may go off.

A tornado races across this open field. Scientists try to find out how fast it is moving, how big it is, and which way it will go next.

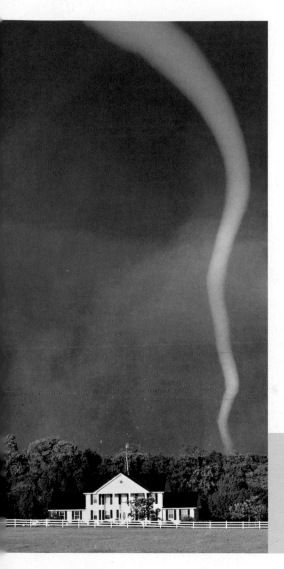

How do people stay safe from a tornado? They watch for thunderstorms and funnel clouds hanging down. They check for warnings. They listen for sirens.

If a tornado is coming, people take shelter. They leave their cars. They try to stay inside and away from windows. They might hide under a strong table.

This tornado has just destroyed one house and is headed toward another. After being warned, the people moved to a safe place.

The safest place to be is in a basement. Some people stay in underground rooms, called storm cellars.

Tornadoes are scary. With enough warning, we can stay safe from these powerful storms!

This woman watches dark storm clouds come closer. Her storm cellar will keep her safe.

Glossary

funnel — a tube that has a wide top and narrow bottom. A tornado is shaped like a funnel.

gas — a form that something can take, such as water. Unlike a solid, a gas cannot hold its own shape. It keeps spreading out. Usually, a gas cannot be seen.

hail — pieces of ice that fall from storm clouds

radar — a machine that shows where things are in a certain place

thunderstorms — heavy rainstorms with thunder and lightning

vacuum cleaner — a machine that cleans carpets and floors by sucking up dirt and other objects

vapor — something that is in a gas form

waterspout — a tube of swirling wind and water that forms when a tornado funnel passes over a lake or sea

For More Information

Books

Tornadoes. Seymour Simon (Sagebrush)

Tornadoes. Extreme Weather (series). Liza N. Burby (PowerKids Press)

Tornadoes. What on Earth? (series). David Orme and Helen Orme (Children's Press)

Wind. Weather Around You (series). Anita Ganeri (Gareth Stevens Publishing)

Web Sites

Forces of Nature: Tornadoes

www.nationalgeographic.com/forcesofnature

This interactive site lets you create your own tornado!

Tornadoes

www.fema.gov/kids/tornado.htm

Read first-hand stories from kids about tornadoes.

Publisher's note to educators and parents: Our editors have carefully reviewed these Web sites to ensure that it is suitable for children. Many Web sites change frequently, however, and we cannot guarantee that a site's future contents will continue to meet our high standards of quality and educational value. Be advised that children should be closely supervised whenever they access the Internet.

Index

About the Author

Jim Mezzanotte has written many books for children. He lives in Milwaukee, Wisconsin, with his wife and two sons. He has always been interested in the weather, especially big storms.